ALTO SAX 1

THE BEST OF
ESSENTIAL ELEMENTS

FOR JAZZ ENSEMBLE

15 ARRANGEMENTS FOR YOUNG JAZZ ENSEMBLE

ISBN-13: 978-1-4234-5215-7
ISBN-10: 1-4234-5215-1

HAL•LEONARD®
CORPORATION

7777 W. BLUEMOUND RD. P.O. BOX 13819 MILWAUKEE, WI 53213

Visit Hal Leonard Online at
www.halleonard.com

ALL OF ME

Words and Music by
SEYMOUR SIMONS and **GERALD MARKS**
Arranged by MICHAEL SWEENEY

Alto Sax I

ALTO SAX

Rhythm Workout

Bah   Doo Dot   Doo Bah Dot   Doo   Doo Dot

Bah   Doo Dot   Dot Doo Bah Dit   Doo   Doo Bah Doo Bah____

Melody Workout

Chord/Scale Workout

Demonstration Solo

MISTER COOL

ALTO SAX I

By Mike Steinel

ALTO SAX

JA-DA

ALTO SAX I

Words and Music by BOB CARLETON
Arranged by MICHAEL SWEENEY

ALTO SAX

Rhythm Workout

Melody Workout

Improvising On The Melody There are many ways to change a melody to create an improvisation.

CHANGING RHYTHMS

REPEATING PARTS OF THE MELODY

FILLING IN THE SKIPS

Demonstration Solo

SONG FOR SAN MIGUEL

Alto Sax 1

By MIKE STEINEL

ALTO SAX

SUNDAY AFTERNOON

ALTO SAX I

By MIKE STEINEL

ALTO SAX

Rhythm Workout

Melody Workout

Scale Workout

Demonstration Solo

TAKE THE "A" TRAIN

Alto Sax 1

Words and Music by
BILLY STRAYHORN

Arranged by MICHAEL SWEENEY

ALTO SAX

Rhythm Workout

Melody Workout

Chord/Scale Workout

Demonstration Solo

BUBBERT'S GROOVE

ALTO SAX 1

By MIKE STEINEL

ALTO SAX

Rhythm Workout

Doo Dot   Doo Dit   Doo   Doo Bah   Dot   Doo Bah   Doo Dot

Doo Dit   Doo   Doo   Doo   Doo   Doo Bah

Melody Workout

Chord/Scale Workout

Demonstration Solo

PERFIDIA

ALTO SAX I

Words and Music by
ALBERTO DOMINGUEZ
Arranged by MICHAEL SWEENEY

ALTO SAX

Rhythm Workout

Dit Doo___ Doo Doo Doo Doo Doo Doo Doo Doo___

Doo Doo Doo Doo Doo Doo Doo Doo Doo___ Doo Doo Doo Doo Doo Doo

Melody Workout

Chord/Scale Workout (Concert B-flat)

Demonstration Solo

BALLAD FOR A BLUE HORN
(Feature for Trumpet or Alto Sax)

Alto Sax 1

By MIKE STEINEL

ALTO SAX

Rhythm Workout – (articulate lightly)

Melody Workout

Helpful Hint: Interpreting solo passages in jazz

Often we are asked to play a "solo" in a jazz piece that is not improvised but rather interpreted in a personal style ("stylized"). In these situations try to maintain the basic melody notes and focus on varying the rhythm of the written part. The demonstration solo is a good example of this technique.

Demonstration Solo – ("Stylized" treatment of melody m. 5-20)

SATIN DOLL

ALTO SAX I

By Duke Ellington
Arranged by MICHAEL SWEENEY

ALTO SAX

SO WHAT

Alto Sax 1

By MILES DAVIS
Arranged by MICHAEL SWEENEY

ALTO SAX

Rhythm Workout

Bah Doo Bah Doo Bah Doo Bah   Doo   Bah Doo Bah Doo Bah Doo Bah   Doo Bah

Melody Workout (A Guide for Improvising)

Scale Workout #1 – Concert D Dorian Scale

Scale Workout #2 – Concert E♭ Dorian Scale

Demonstration Solo

BUBBERT GOES RETRO

Alto Sax 1

By Mike Steinel

ALTO SAX

BASIN STREET BLUES

Alto Sax 1

Words and Music by
SPENCER WILLIAMS
Arranged by MICHAEL SWEENEY

ALTO SAX

ON BROADWAY

Alto Sax 1

Words and Music by BARRY MANN,
CYNTHIA WEIL, MIKE STOLLER and JERRY LEIBER
Arranged by MICHAEL SWEENEY

ALTO SAX

Rhythm Workout

Doo Doo Doo Doo Bah   Doo   Doo Bah   Dit   Doo   Bah

Doo Doo Doo Doo Bah   Doo   Doo Bah   Doo Doo   Doo

Melody Workout

Scale Workout

MIXOLYDIAN SCALE

"MAJOR" BLUES SCALE

Demonstration Solo

BLUES FOR A NEW DAY

Alto Sax 1

By MIKE STEINEL

ALTO SAX

Rhythm Workout

Bah Doo Bah Doo Doo Bah   Doo Dot   Bah Doo Bah Doo Bah

Doo Bah Doo Bah   Doo Bah   Bah Doo Dot   Bah Doo Bah Doo Bah   Doo Bah Doo Bah   Doo Dot

Melody Workout

Scale Workout

Demonstration Solo